FUN BOOK

Dedicated to
Oisín and Zoë

Also by Don Conroy

- *The Fox's Tale*
- *What the Owl Saw*

- *Mumbo & Jumbo's Big Break*
- *The Anaconda from Drumcondra*
- *Elephant at the Door*
- *The Bookworm Who Turned Over
  A New Leaf*
- *Rocky The Dinosaur*
- *Seal of Approval*

- *Vampire Journal*
- *Vampire of St Michan's*

- *Wildlife Colouring & Activity Book*
- *Rocky's Fun Book*
- *Cartoon Crazy*

TRAVEL
FUN BOOK

Written and illustrated by

DON CONROY

POOLBEG
FOR CHILDREN

Published 2002
by Poolbeg Press Ltd
123 Grange Hill, Baldoyle
Dublin 13, Ireland
E-mail: poolbeg@poolbeg.com

1 3 5 7 9 10 8 6 4 2

A catalogue record for this book is available from the British Library.

ISBN 1 -84223-005-0

Cover design by Steven Hope
Illustrations by Don Conroy
Typeset by Patricia Hope
Printed by
Cox and Wyman

www.poolbeg.com

A Book in the Post

It was a cold wet Monday morning in October. Having reluctantly left a warm bed I peered out the window of my bedroom. The rain was beating against the glass and large puddles were forming in a dip in the road. I washed, got dressed and brushed my teeth, then headed down the stairs. My mother was in the kitchen listening to the radio and making my lunch.

A loud knock at the hall door stopped me in my tracks. I then hurried down the rest of the stairs and, reaching up, pulled across the bolt and opened the door. There stood our tall, very wet, postman Peter. No Postman Pat here! Peter was one of the grumpiest people one could meet, a bad weather face come rain or shine. I imagined he must have looked in the mirror each morning to check and chase away any hint of a friendly smile. Once secure in the knowledge that he had a scowl showing he headed off to work contented.

Through narrow turned down lips he snapped: "A parcel for Donal Conroy."

I looked at him in amazement. Rain was running down his face, gathering around his hooked nose and forming a large drop waiting to fall at any second. He never wore a cap or hat; he seemed very proud of his black wavy hair. Water separated into drops on the heavy brylcreem-ed hair and ran down on to his collar, like water off a duck's back.

"I am at the right house?" he glared.

"Of yes, of course," I blurted.

My mother arrived on the scene and made a comment about him having to walk around in this weather. He agreed as she signed for the parcel.

"It's for you," she said to me.

I nodded excitedly. I couldn't understand who would be sending me a present, for my birthday was in June. I didn't know anyone in England at the time. You see, I knew it was from England because of the stamps showing a profile of the queen. Then it clicked. The queen must have sent it to me.

I suggested this explanation to my mother who laughed. "I don't think the queen would be writing to you somehow."

I quickly tore open the brown paper wrapping having removed the string first. Inside was a magnificent coffee-table-sized book entitled the Wildlife of Britain and Ireland. My eyes widened. I opened a page at random. There were wonderful photographs, and drawings of badgers and foxes. Some pages had full pages of paintings of owls and eagles. I was delighted but baffled as to who might have sent it to me.

My mother checked inside the cover. There was an inscription

To Donal Conroy
1st Prize in the
Shell Art Competition

I was very excited and pleased with myself. But then began to panic. I hadn't entered the competition so how could I have won? Would I have to send the book back?

"I know what happened," said my mother calmly. "Remember the painting you sent to Aunt Elizabeth (not the queen, she is Elizabeth too!) of the robin. She must have entered it into the competition for you and that's how you won the prize."

I later found out that that was exactly what had happened.

I carefully packed the book in my school bag to protect it from the elements and headed for school. Having spent all the bus journey looking at the book I nearly missed the stop where I was to get off. When I arrived in the class I was early, the teacher was not there yet, so I took out the book to show it off to my friends and explained how I had come by it.

"You won that!" exclaimed one.

"You're brilliant at drawing," said another.

I beamed proudly as, lying across a desk, we poured over its contents.

Our teacher, Brother X, stormed into the class like a whirlwind. Brother X was a very tall thin man with wiry red hair that stood up like Bart Simpson's head. It looked like his head was on fire, and he always spoke as if his trousers were on fire too.

"I heard noise coming up the corridor," he bellowed. He stood there like a gunslinger from an old western movie, with his leather strap sticking out from his black trousers pocket.

I quickly hid the book behind my back and backed away to my desk. His eyes scanned the pupils. Then they stopped at me. They seemed to bore into me.

"What's behind yer back?" he yelled. "I hope it's a school book because if it's not I'll flay you alive."

That was an unfortunate expression to use on a nine-year-old boy with a vivid imagination, who believed his teacher was capable of anything. It didn't help matters either that the same boy had recently seen an old movie called Zarak at the Sunday matinee in the local cinema, where the hero Victor Mature gets flayed alive by Afghanistan rebels, because he saved the British troops from being massacred.

I trembled and stared back, opened my mouth but no words came out.

One of my friends immediately jumped to my

rescue waving his right hand in the air. "Please sir, Don won a book in an art competition in England! First Prize!"

The teacher glared at him then looked back at me. "Show me it," he demanded. His tone seemed softer. As I produced the book some of my class mates removed their hands from the radiator, in the knowledge that all was safe. The trick was to heat your hands on the radiator before you were beaten with the leather strap. That way the pain was somewhat reduced, for to be hit hard on cold hands was the worst of all.

No leather was used that day. I was asked to stand up in front of the class and read aloud sections about birds and animals to the class. That afternoon some of my friends and I met at my pal David's house, whose Mum was a fantastic cook and always produced hot apple tart and ice cream for us, and tea.

While we were there we decided to start a Wildlife Club and it was all because of this amazing book I had received in the post.

CUSTER'S LAST STAND

Major General George Armstrong Custer and the United States 7th Cavalry were wiped out at the Battle of Little Big-Horn, by Chief Crazy Horse and his Oglala tribe along with Sitting Bull and the Hunkpapa. Other tribes that fought in this fierce battle were the Cheyenne, Arapaho, Blackfeet, Minecojou and Sans Arc.

Some of the soldiers were from Ireland, the most well known was Lieutenant Myles Keogh from Co. Wexford. The battle took place in the Black Hills of Montana on June 25th 1876.

The only survivor of the entire battalion was a horse called Comanche.

A VISION OF VICTORY

Sitting Bull, the holy man of the Hunkpapa Sioux, had watched the terrible slaughter of the buffalo by the whites. He realised that this would bring famine to his people. So he tried to rally the tribes against the whites. In a vision at the sun-dance ceremony he saw soldiers upside down. At the Battle of Little Big-Horn they fought against the 7th Cavalry and won. Sitting Bull's vision had come true.

"I AM HERE BY THE WILL OF THE GREAT SPIRIT AND BY HIS WILL I AM CHIEF"

SITTING BULL 1831–1890
CHIEF OF THE HUNKPAPA SIOUX

JOKES

❋ Why did the man call his dog 'Camera'?
Because it was always snapping.

❋ Did you hear about the man who does bird impressions?
He eats worms.

❋ The teacher asks the class during a visit to a nature reserve: 'How can one tell a weasel from a stoat?'
A boy replied: 'A weasel is weasily recognised but a stoat is stotally different.'

❋ What do you get if you cross a goat with an owl?
A hooting nanny.

❋ An absent-minded farmer fed his hens on sawdust instead of grain.
When the hens laid eggs they hatched out woodpeckers.

STRANGE BUT TRUE

The man who created Dracula was an Irishman.

Probably the most famous gothic novel of all time, and it was written by Irishman, Bram Stoker.

Who was Bram Stoker?

The somewhat forgotten man of Irish literature, Bram (Abraham) Stoker, was born in Clontarf, Dublin, Ireland in November 1847. Stoker, the author of the world's biggest-selling novel, Dracula, had a sickly childhood but later grew strong and became very athletic as he got older. After completing a degree course at Trinity College. He then followed in his father's

Bram Stoker

footsteps into the civil service at Dublin Castle.

Stoker had a keen interest in the theatre and during the 1870's he wrote a drama review column for Dublin's Daily Mail newspaper. This work greatly contributed to the nurturing of the dramatic scene in Dublin and helped pave the way for the founding of the National Theatre later.

In 1878 Stoker married Florence Balcombe who

had been courted by Oscar Wilde and moved to England where he became secretary to his great acting idol Henry Irving and manager of Irving's Lyceum Theatre in London.

Stoker remained with Irving until the actor's death in 1905 and under his direction Henry became the first actor to be knighted. Bram Stoker died in London 1912. He was survived by his wife Florence and their only child Noel (b. 1879).

The Dracula legacy
Bram Stoker wrote some 18 books and a myriad of shorter works of fiction and non-fiction. The book that immortalised him, the world famous masterpiece of gothic horror, Dracula, was first published in 1897. The success of this vampire novel is unlikely ever to be equalled. Indeed it has totally eclipsed Stoker himself.

The book has never been out of print and is the biggest-selling novel ever written. The only book to sell more copies is The Bible! Dracula has been translated into all the world's major languages and many minor ones. Over 700 films have been based on it. In the worlds of cinema, theatre, art and the performing arts in general and the literary world it continues to inspire countless new creative works.

Can you help Al the Anaconda find his way home?

AL'S HOME

Questions

1. What is a buzzard?

2. What bird is called a butcher-bird?

3. What is a butterworth?

4. What is a baboon?

5. What is an armadillo?

6. What is a blenny?

7. What is a boa?

8. What is a bobcat?

Answers on next page

Answers

1. A large bird of prey found in Europe.

2. The shrike, which impales insects etc. on thorns.

3. An insect-eating plant of bogs and marshes.

4. A primate found in Africa, that lives in highly organised family groups.

5. An armoured omnivorous animal found in USA, Mexico and South America.

6. A small fish found in rock pools.

7. A large snake found in South America, which kills its prey by coiling around the victim, then suffocating it.

8. A wildcat found in USA, Canada and Mexico, also known as a lynx.

Questions

1. What is the largest animal that ever lived?

2. Do bird-eating spiders really eat birds?

3. What is a birdwing?

4. What is a bracken?

5. What is a bison?

6. What is a condor?

7. What is a conger?

8. What is a gila monster?

Answers on next page

Answers

1. The blue whale. It may grow up to 30 metres. Rare but thankfully still survives in our oceans.

2. Yes. They chase after prey as they do not make webs. Their bodies are covered with poisonous hairs.

3. A beautiful butterfly found in the forests of South-east Asia.

4. A species of fern.

5. A massive ox-like mammal found in Europe and America. Also called a buffalo or wisent.

6. A vulture. There are two species, the Andean and the rare Californian.

7. A stout-bodied marine eel, up to 2.5 metres long.

8. A poisonous lizard found in the desert in South-west America.

Questions

1. What is a red jungle fowl?

2. What bird in Britain and Ireland has the shortest name?

3. What is 'injury-feigning' in birds?

4. What is camouflage?

5. What is a purple hairstreak?

6. What does the term 'vagrant' mean?

7. What are invertebrates?

8. What is a hybrid?

Answers on next page

Answers

1. A bird found in the Himalayas. A close relative of the pheasant, our domestic chickens were bred from them.

2. The jay (a member of the crow family).

3. A special trick used by birds to lead predators away from eggs or chicks.

4. Special colours or patterns to help make a creature more difficult to see.

5. A butterfly.

6. A bird that is somewhere it shouldn't be.

7. Creatures without backbones e.g. worms.

8. A cross between two species.

Questions

1. What is a golden eagle's nest called?

2. What is a very young golden eagle called?

3. What liquid was also named Adam's Ale?

4. What is the name for frozen dew?

5. What is guano?

6. What does the term game bird mean?

7. What is 'home range'?

8. What is 'display' in birds?

Answers on next page

Answers

1. An eyrie.

2. An eaglet.

3. Water.

4. Hoar-frost.

5. Sea-bird droppings, which accumulate in the one area over many years.

6. A word to describe pheasants, partridges, grouse and their relatives which are shot for sport.

7. The area occupied by a bird or a pair of birds (e.g. the home range of the golden eagle).

8. Signals between birds e.g. threat display, submission, courtship etc.

First man: 'I'm glad I wasn't born in Russia.'
Second man: 'Why?'
First man: 'Because I can't speak Russian.'

First man: 'My wife's so graceful, she just glides into a room.'
Second man: 'Yes, I've seen her on the skateboard.'

❉ What's the moon's favourite music?
Loony tunes.

❉ My apartment is so small I have to buy condensed milk.

❉ Did you hear about the boy that was named after his father?
They call him 'Dad'.

Mum: 'Don't come in with filthy feet.'
Son: 'But my feet are clean, it's only my boots that are dirty.'

First farmer: 'On my farm I can produce eggs without hens.'
Second farmer: 'That's amazing, how do you manage it?'
First farmer: 'Easy. I keep ducks.'

A wife asked her husband if he thought her singing voice was improving.
'Yes,' he replied, 'but it's not cured.'

GENERAL KNOWLEDGE QUIZ

Questions

1. What is a nimbus?

2. In the Northern Hemisphere when is the summer solstice?

3. Name the seven seas (oceans).

4. What type of clouds are associated with thunderstorms?

5. How is thunder produced?

6. If you were to look at a snowflake under a microscope, how many star-points would it have: 4, 6 or 8?

7. Where does a hurricane begin: over land or over sea?

8. What is a tornado?

Answers on next page

Answers

1. A rain-cloud (usually with ragged edges).

2. June 21st

3. i. North Atlantic ii. South Atlantic
   iii. North Pacific iv. South Pacific
   v. Indian Ocean vi. Arctic vii. Antarctic

4. Cumulonimbus clouds.

5. Thunder is produced by the rapid expansion of air when heated by lightning.

6. Six.

7. Over sea.

8. An extreme form of cyclone that begins over land.

Questions

1. Do planets give out light?

2. Where is the Sea of Tranquillity situated?

3. What is a super nova?

4. Do stars give out light?

5. What planet is called the 'Morning Star' or the 'Evening Star'?

6. When was Halley's Comet last seen in our skies: 1976, 1986, 1996?

7. In what galaxy is the earth situated?

Answers on next page

Answers

1. No. They reflect sunlight.

2. On the surface of the moon.

3. An exploding star.

4. Yes, stars burn white-hot giving out their own light.

5. Venus.

6. 1986. It returns every 76 years. Next sighting 2062.

7. The Milky Way.

Questions

1. What is the largest organ in the body (excluding skin)?

2. In the human body, where would you find these bones: the femur, tibia and fibula. Is it the arm, the leg or the backbone?

3. What is arachnophobia?

4. Both male and female bees and wasps sting. True or false?

5. Who was the first president of the USA?

6. Which country drinks the most tea per head of population. Is it England, Ireland or India?

7. Where is the largest library in the world?

8. What is the tallest species of tree?

9. Where is the least amount of sunshine in the world?

10. Who was the first man to walk on the moon?

11. Where is the Simpson desert?

12. What is the difference between the bactrian and the dromedary camel?

Answers on next page

Answers

1. The liver.
2. The leg.
3. A fear of spiders.
4. False, only the females sting.
5. George Washington (1789-97)
6. Ireland.
7. The Library of Congress, Washington DC.
It has 29 million books.
8. The eucalyptus tree of Australia. 114m.
(374 ft.)
9. The South Pole. It has 182 days of darkness.
10. Neil Armstrong (USA) in 1969.
11. In Australia.
12. Bactrian camels have two humps and are still found in the wild. Dromedary camels only have one hump.

Questions

1. Where is St Peter's, Vatican City?

2. Where do the Lapp people live?

3. Where did the Vikings come from?

4. What is the capital of Belgium?

5. What is the highest point in Ireland?

6. What is the highest point in the United Kingdom?

7. When was the French Revolution? Was it 1789, 1798 or 1814?

8. What ocean is off the coast of Portugal?

Answers on next page

Answers

1. Rome, Italy.

2. Lapland.

3. Scandinavia.

4. Brussels.

5. Carrantouhill (1042m)

6. Ben Nevis (1347m)

7. 1789

8. Atlantic Ocean.

Questions

1. What is the capital of Spain?

2. What are the colours of the Spanish flag?

3. What is the capital of Italy?

4. What is the capital of Malta?

5. What is the capital of Poland?

6. What is the capital of Hungary?

7. What is the capital of Scotland?

8. Where is Transylvania?

Answers on next page

Answers

1. Madrid.

2. Red and yellow.

3. Rome.

4. Valletta.

5. Warsaw.

6. Budapest.

7. Edinburgh.

8. Romania.

Questions

1. Name the nine planets in our solar system.

2. What is the largest desert in the world?

3. Which is the largest lake in the world? Is it the Caspian, Superior, Victoria, Aral, or the Huron?

4. What is the longest river in the world?

5. What is the highest waterfall in the world?

6. What is the largest island in the world? Is it Great Britain, Madagascar, Sumatra, Borneo or Greenland?

7. What is the highest mountain in the world?

Answers on next page

33

Answers

1. Mercury, Venus, Earth, Mars, Jupiter, Saturn, Uranus, Neptune, Pluto.

2. The Sahara. 8,400,000 sq. km.

3. The Caspian 'Sea'. 438,695 sq. km.

4. The Nile (Africa). 6677 km.

5. Angel Falls (Venezuela). 979 metres.

6. Greenland (North Atlantic). 2,175,600 sq. km.

7. Mount Everest (Himalayas - Nepal).

GENERAL QUIZ: IRELAND

1. What is the largest island off the coast of Ireland?

2. Name the three main Aran islands.

3. In what county is Errigal mountain located?

4. What is the name of the most northerly point of mainland Ireland?

5. Name the Shannon's three major lakes?

6. What is peat?

7. This well known verse of prophesy 'one for sorrow, two for joy' is associated with which bird?

8. Which Irish county has the shortest coastline?

9. What is a coppice?

10. What is a runnel?

11. What is the national emblem of Ireland: the harp, the shamrock or the castle?

12. Is ice more or less dense than water?

13. What percentage of cow's milk is water: 20%, 87% or 70%.

14. What is the ozone layer?

15. Which is the brightest of the fixed stars?

Answers

1. Achill.

2. Inishmore, Inishmann, Inisheer.

3. Co. Donegal.

4. Malin Head (Co. Donegal)

5. Loughs Allen, Ree and Derg.

6. Decayed and partly carbonized vegetable matter found in boglands.

7. The magpie.

8. Co. Leitrim.

9. A wood, thicket or small plantation of trees.

10. A small stream or brook.

11. The harp.

12. Less.

13. 87%.

14. A narrow layer of ozone gas that protects the earth from harmful ultra-violet rays.

15. Sirius - the dog star.

Amazing facts about our Solar System

- The hottest planet is Venus due to its proximity to the Sun.
- The fastest-moving planet is Mercury orbiting at 107030 mph (172248 km/h).
- The longest day on a planet is on Venus. It rotates backwards on its axis, once every 243 days.
- The brightest planet is Venus. It reflects 79% of its incoming light from the sun.
- The largest known volcano on a planet is Olympus Mons. Found on Mars. 375 miles (600 km) across and 15 miles high (25km).
- Saturn has the largest rings around it. 170,000 miles (270,000 km) in diameter.
- The coldest place in our solar system is Neptune's moon 'Triton' with temperatures of -235 degrees celsius
- Planet Earth is the third planet from our sun. The distance is 94,450,000 miles (152,000,000 km).

- Our moon is 238828 miles (384400 km) from planet Earth.
- The surface shapes on the moon are mainly due to meteorite impacts.
- The moon is moving away from the earth at a rate of 4cm (1.5 inches) a year.
- The asteroid belt is found between Mars and Jupiter.
- There are at least 1 million asteroids in our solar system.
- The largest known asteroid is called 'Ceres', with a diameter of 584 miles (940km).
- The largest crater found on the surface of our Earth caused by a meteorite impact is in Arizona USA. Discovered in 1871, its diameter is 4150ft (1265m).
- Comets are large dirty snowballs made of rock, dust and ice.
- Halley's Comet was first discovered in 239 BC. It's seen in our solar system once every 76 years.

Questions

1. What is a hawksbill?

2. What is heather?

3. What is a hermit crab?

4. What is a hobby?

5. What is hogweed?

6. What is a hoopoe?

7. What is a koala?

8. What is a krill?

Answers on next page

Answers

1. A small turtle with a hooked bill.
2. A low evergreen shrub with purple flowers, found on heaths, moorlands and boglands.
3. A crab that lives in the empty shell of another creature such as a whelk or winkle.
4. A small falcon.
5. A large coarse plant of the parsley family.
6. A bird with a fan-shaped crest. Its name is derived from its call.
7. A 'bear-like' pouched animal, but not a bear. Found in Australia, related to the possum, feeds mainly on eucalyptus leaves.
8. A tiny shrimp-like creature found in the sea. A favourite food for baleen whales.

Questions

1. What is a kite?

2. What is a musk ox?

3. What is a muntjac?

4. What is a nuthatch?

5. How many arms has an octopus: 6,8 or 12?

6. What is an okapi?

7. What creature is called 'the old man of the forest'?

8. What is a coypu?

Answers on next page

Answers

1. A bird of prey with a forked tail and long pointed wings.
2. A large bulky animal that lives on the bleak tundra of Alaska, Canada and Greenland.
3. A small deer found in South-east Asia.
4. A small bird which crawls up and down in tree-trunks.
5. Eight.
6. An African animal related to the giraffe.
7. The orang-utan, an ape found in the forests of Borneo and Sumatra.
8. A large rodent, native to the swamps of South America.

Questions

1. What is a copperhead?

2. The mountain lion of North America is also known by two other names. What are they?

3. What is a coyote?

4. What is a lotus?

5. What is a lorikeet?

6. What is a llama?

7. What is a seahorse?

8. What is a sidewinder?

Answers on next page

Answers

1. A small venomous snake found in Australia.
2. Puma or cougar.
3. A small wolf.
4. A kind of water-lily.
5. A colourful little parrot found in Australia and the South Pacific.
6. A South American relative of the camel.
7. A small fish found in coastal waters.
8. A rattlesnake found in the deserts of North America.

Questions

1. What is a terrapin?

2. What is a thresher?

3. What is a tetrapod?

4. What is 'tree of heaven'?

5. What is bird's-foot trefoil?

6. What is a trogan?

7. What is a tree fern?

8. What is a sturgeon?

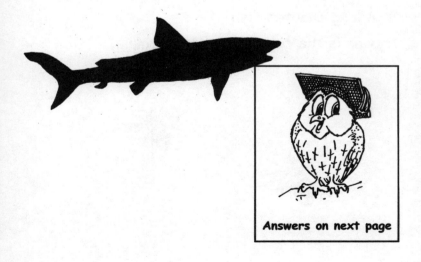

Answers on next page

Answers

1. A tortoise found in estuaries in North America and Mexico.
2. A type of shark.
3. A term applied to any four-footed animal.
4. A fast-growing Chinese tree also known as ailanthus.
5. A red-tinged yellow flower of the clover family.
6. A brightly coloured bird found in Central America.
7. A large series of fern that grows to 12 metres tall (resembles a palm tree).
8. A long-snouted fish (caviar is the egg-mass of the female).

Questions

1. What is a stork?

2. What is a reed?

3. What is a cat-bear?

4. What is a ratel?

5. What is a red admiral?

6. Why is the rattlesnake so named?

7. What is a redwood?

8. Where are rhesus monkeys found?

Answers on next page

47

Answers

1. A large black and white bird found in marshes in most parts of the world.
2. Any slender tall plant found growing in shallow ponds or swamps.
3. The red panda. Lives in the Himalayas. Feeds on fruits and berries.
4. A black and white badger-like animal, relative of the wolverine. Found in Africa and India. Also known as the honey badger.
5. A migratory butterfly.
6. It rattles when disturbed. This sound is produced by the horny rings on the tail.
7. A large coniferous tree of the western United States. Grows up to 90 metres.
Also known as the sequoias.
8. India and South-east Asia. When frightened their faces turn red.

Questions

1. What is a flying fox?

2. What is frogmouth?

3. What is a rhea?

4. What is a roach?

5. What is a roadrunner?

6. Why was the right whale so named?

7. What is a rifleman?

8. What is a roller?

9. What is a beluga?

Answers on next page

49

Answers

1. A fruit bat.
2. A bird of the night with a frog-like gape found in South-east Asia and Australia.
3. A flightless ostrich-like bird found in South America.
4. A common freshwater fish found in Europe and Asia.
5. A cuckoo found in the deserts of North America.
6. Whalers hunting this whale named it the 'right' whale because it didn't sink when harpooned.
7. A New Zealand wren with a long needle-like bill.
8. A jay-like bird found in Africa.
9. A white whale relative of the dolphin and porpoise.

GENERAL KNOWLEDGE QUIZ

Questions

1. Who is regarded as one of the greatest intellects in the history of mankind (renowned for the theory of relativity)?

2. Name the famous American writer of the macabre whose grandparents came from Kildallon, Co. Cavan?

3. What is another name for a hoverfly?

4. Did St Patrick really banish the snakes from Ireland?

5. In Greek mythology nectar is the drink of the gods. What is it?

6. The month of May is named after the Greek goddess of nature, what was her name?

7. In Greek mythology what birds were Halcyon and Ceyx turned into?

8. In Greek mythology Aeolus was the god of what?

9. In Irish mythology who was Oisin's father?

Answers on next page

Answers

1. Albert Einstein.

2. Edgar Allen Poe.

3. A dronefly.

4. No - there are no records of indigenous snakes ever having occurred in Ireland.

5. Saccharine substance secreted from some plants - also called honey.

6. Maia.

7. Kingfishers (once believed to make a floating nest in the sea which remained calm during hatching, hence the expression 'halcyon days' of peace and happiness).

8. The wind.

9. Fionn Mac Cumhall.

Questions

1. What is a backswimmer?

2. What is a babbler?

3. Where would one find a bower bird?

4. What is a box?

5. What is a penny bolete?

6. What is a booby?

7. What is a hellbender?

8. What is cross-pollination?

Answers on next page

Answers

1. A waterbug that swims upside down using its long handles as oars.
2. A name given to birds with loud and varied calls which usually live on the forest floor of Australia, South-east Asia and North America.
3. In Australia and North Guinea.
4. A slow-growing evergreen tree found in Europe, Asia and North Africa.
5. A fleshy fungi that is edible and used to make mushroom soup.
6. A group of birds related to the gannet.
7. A giant salamander (up to 75cm) found in the fast-flowing streams of the Eastern United States, also in China and Japan.
8. The transfer of pollen from one species to another.

Questions

1. What is crowfoot?

2. What are curassow?

3. What common plant was once known as 'day's eye'?

4. What is the common name for animals bearing antlers rather than horns?

5. What is a dead-nettle?

6. What creature is known as the devil's coach-horse?

7. What is a Rocky Mountain goat?

8. What is a stinkhorn?

Answers on next page

Answers

1. An aquatic plant of the buttercup family.
2. A small group of birds with 'horny' helmets found in Central and South America, pheasant or turkey size.
3. The daisy, so called because it closes up at night or on dull days.
4. Deer (ruminants).
5. A herb that looks similar to the nettle but does not sting.
6. The rove beetle, a black beetle found in damp places (length 2.5cm).
7. A goat-antelope found in the mountain regions of North America. Usually has white hair and curved horns.
8. A foul-smelling fungus that attracts flies which help the fungus to transfer its spores to other locations.

Questions

1. What is the largest shark in the world?

2. What is a wombat?

3. What is a glutton?

4. What is wolfsbane?

5. What is a wobbegong?

6. What is a wrasse?

7. What is wormwood?

8. What is tamarind?

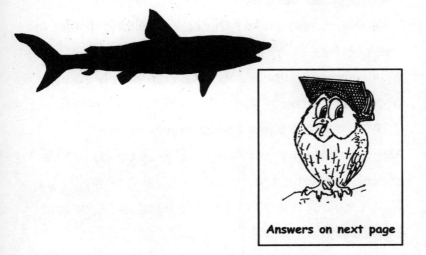

Answers on next page

Answers

1. The whale shark. A harmless shark that feeds on plankton and grows to 15 metres in length.

2. A marsupial that's related to the koala. Entirely vegetarian. Two species found in Australia.

3. Another name for the fierce wolverine, the largest of the weasel family, found in the USA and the Northern European forest.

4. A very poisonous herb related to the buttercup. In past times used to poison wolves or foxes in bait or rubbed on arrows to give them a poisonous tip.

5. A shark, also called the carpet shark, found in the pacific.

6. A brightly coloured marine fish mainly found in tropical waters.

7. A composite plant found mainly in the Northern Hemisphere (over 250 species) with a strong aromatic fragrance.

8. A tropical tree. Its fruit is used in foods and beverages.

JOKES

First boy: 'My dog can jump higher than an elephant.'

Second boy: 'That's amazing! How did you manage that?'

First boy: 'Easy. Elephants can't jump, they're too heavy.'

First man: 'My cat got the first prize at a bird show.'

Second man: 'How come?'

First man: 'It ate the prize canary.'

Patient: 'Doctor, my hair is falling out, can you give me something to keep it in?'

Doctor: 'Sure, here's a paper bag.'

First man: 'You're a doctor of music?'

Second man, beaming proudly: 'Yes!'

First man: 'Can you fix my piano? It has a broken leg.'

Man: I know two words in every language.

Girl: What are they?

'Coca Cola'

AMAZING FACTS ABOUT REPTILES

* Snakes and lizards grow throughout their lives.
* Sea turtles may lay up to two hundred eggs in one clutch.
* The largest reptile is the saltwater crocodile which can grow up to 7m (23ft.)
* The smallest reptile is a species of gecko found on the Virgin Islands 3.5cm (1.4 inches)
* The longest-living reptiles are turtles and tortoises. Records of 152 years.
* The fastest snake in the world is the black mamba. It can move at speeds up to 19km/h (12mph)
* The largest lizard is the komodo dragon found in Indonesia. It can grow up to 3m (9.8ft.)
* The longest snake is the reticulated python. Most average 6.25m (20.5ft.)

REPTILE QUIZ

Which is the odd one out?

- crocodile
- snake
- lizard
- frog
- turtle
- slow worm

The frog is an amphibian while
the rest are reptiles.

★ Do reptiles lay eggs or give birth
to live young?
Some reptiles give birth to live young e.g.
common lizard, adder. Others, like grass snakes
and crocodiles, lay eggs.

★ Young reptiles are called tadpoles.
True or false?
False. Young amphibians (larvae) e.g. frog, newt,
are called tadpoles.

★ Snakes can blink. True or false?
False. Snakes have no eyelids, though lizards
have.

★ Snakes are found in Britain and Ireland.
True or false?
False. There are no snakes in Ireland. Britain
has three species of snake: adder, grass and
smooth.

DINOSAUR FACTS

TOP 10 LONGEST DINOSAURS

		Meaning	Metres
1	Seismosaurus	earth-shaking lizard	40
2	Supersaurus	super lizard	30
3	Barosaurus	heavy lizard	27
4	Diplodocus	double beam	27
5	Ultrasaurus	ultra lizard	27
6	Brachiosaurus	arm lizard	25
7	Mamenchisaurus	mamen brook lizard	25
8	Pelorosaurus	monstrous lizard	24
9	Apatosaurus	deceptive lizard	21
10	Camarasaurus	chambered lizard	18

Can you help the elephant find
his way to the bunch of
bananas?

Let's draw a robin

Fig 1 With a soft pencil (HB or 2B) draw the egg shapes as shown. Indicate bill, eye, tail and legs

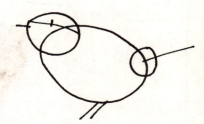

Fig 2 Work up shape of Robin around the egg shapes adding more detail

Fig 3 When satisfied with shape and form of the robin go over pencil lines with felt-tipped pen. When dry, rub out unwanted pencil lines. Using hatching and dots complete drawing

Colour the robin

Let's draw a horse

How to draw a horse's head in three easy steps

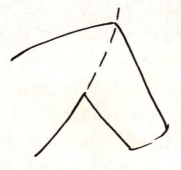

Fig 1 Roughly sketch head and neck with a pencil

Fig 2 Work up head shape as shown

Fig 3 Finish sketch with added detail. Put in with a fine felt tipped pen

Some ancient cultures believed, if you dreamt of animals, that these were symbols and by understanding these symbols you could crack the code of your dreams. See below some of these symbolic representations.

Cats	hidden things
Birds	dreaming
Crows	omens of evil
Dragons	power, magic, eternity
Monsters	fear
Spiders	wisdom
Toads	change
Gardens	birth of a baby
Flowers	a marriage
Wolves	death

ALIENS

Down through the ages there are people who believe that they have contacted aliens and others who claim they have been abducted by them (the first are known as 'contactees' and the latter 'abductees'). They claim a multitude of 'alien' races exist.

ALIEN FILE

Types of aliens

The Grays

The most common aliens are known as Grays. They belong to a military society. Their aim is universal conquest. The main group appear to be about four and a half feet tall with large heads, black wraparound eyes and slits for mouths.

There are taller groups, almost up to eight feet tall, who appear to be friendlier than the smaller Grays.

The most dangerous are the third group, only three and a half feet tall but otherwise similar to the other groups.

The Reptilians

Genetically related to reptiles these advanced aliens are supposed to have lived on the earth a long time ago. They moved to a distant planet which they eventually destroyed. At present they live on a giant asteroid but want to return to earth - this is their mission.

Human-like aliens

Type A

Handsome human-like aliens called 'blonds', controlled by the Grays. They live among us.

Type B

Similar in appearance to 'blonds', this group are called Pleiadeans. They are highly evolved spiritual beings sometimes referred to as angels. These come to visit the earth on rare occasions to help mankind.

Type C
These are benevolent beings similar in appearance to the Pleiadeans but are from Sirius. Very little is known about these beings but they seem to be here to protect us from other dangerous aliens.

ALIEN SKULL?
A skull found in the ancestral land of the Anasari Indians in the USA showed huge eye-sockets, a small mouth and narrow nasal cavities and appears similar to drawings made by people claiming to be abductees. Medical reports, however, say it was a skull of a child suffering from an unusual congenital bone defect. Maybe. But the Anasari name means 'ancient alien'.

THE GHOST IN THE TOWER
The tower of London is famous for its ghost stories because of its bloodthirsty history. Down

through the centuries dozens of ghosts have been seen by keepers and visitors to the infamous place. The most famous ghost is Anne Boleyn who was married to Henry VIII. He had her beheaded in the tower in 1536. Since then her ghost is supposed to wander the stairs and corridors of the tower. Some people claim they have seen her ghost while others claim to have been touched in the face by the restless spirit. Some even claim to have been pushed down the stairs by the troubled ghost as she searches the tower to take revenge on her husband. I don't think she has a ghost of a chance!

In 1977 spaceships Voyager I and Voyager II were launched. Each carried a gold-coated copper record encased in a durable aluminium jacket. On a twelve-inch piece of metal a special message was carried to the stars. It included hundreds of photographs, detailed road maps, historic buildings and landmarks, dazzling images and 'Greetings to anyone who reads this' in 55 different languages, 90 minutes of a variety of music from classical to pop, native to folk and amazing sounds from our beautiful planet Earth. The records also included a greeting from the former president of the United Nations which said 'I send greetings on behalf of the people of our planet. We step out of our solar system, into the universe seeking only peaceful contact'.

Picture this

Today, if you want to paint a picture, you can go to an art shop and there is a variety of wonderful vibrant paints to choose from: oils, acrylics, gouaches, watercolours, poster paints and of course all those coloured pencils, crayons and pastels. All readymade for you to get started - what a luxury!

It wasn't always as easy as this. When you visit an art gallery and look at the old masters' oil paintings remember things were very different then. Colours were very hard to come by then and only rich people could afford them as coloured paint was mainly made from mineral materials. The artists, who were usually poor people, made their own paints. First they had to get minerals, then grind them up in a pestle to a fine powder, then mix with oil, usually linseed oil or gum (this would help it flow from the brush without it becoming lumpy). Some artists used secret ingredients. They used iron minerals found in the clay to produce yellows, oranges and browns. Colours like green came from copper minerals.

Poisonous arsenic minerals were used to make brilliant yellows or oranges. Vermilion, a rich red was made from mercury minerals and cinnabar. So not only was it hard work to make your paints if you were an artist, it was very dangerous as many of these minerals were poisonous.

The most prized of all pigments was a brilliant blue. Called ultramarine, which means 'beyond the water', in medieval times it was more expensive than using gold. Ultramarine comes from the mineral lazurite. In those days it could only be found in remote mountains in Afghanistan and India. Most poor artists had to use plant material as a poor substitute for their blues.

Imagine you had a time machine and you could bring someone like Michaelangleo or Leonardo de Vinci from then to the present day and show them inside a big art store. Can you imagine how excited they would be? We live in such a colourful world but most of us just take it for granted.

WHALE AND DOLPHIN ANAGRAM QUIZ

1.	kenim lehaw	11. fin whale
2.	tetlob dosen pinhold	10. blue whale
3.	robhura sepopior	9. sperm whale
4.	tilop lawhe	8. right whale
5.	mocomn lipdohn	7. risso's dolphin
6.	lilerk elwha	6. killer whale
7.	sossir poldhin	5. common dolphin
8.	thigr wheal	4. pilot whale
9.	mespr lwahe	3. harbour porpoise
10.	lbeu elwha	2. bottle-nosed dolphin
11.	ifn ewhal	1. minke whale

Let's draw a dolphin

You will need a soft pencil (2B), paper, eraser and felt-tipped pen.

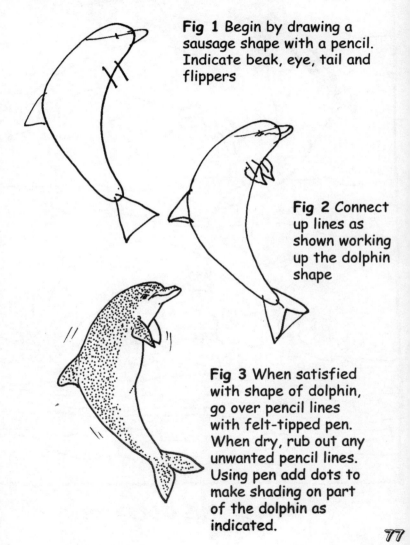

Fig 1 Begin by drawing a sausage shape with a pencil. Indicate beak, eye, tail and flippers

Fig 2 Connect up lines as shown working up the dolphin shape

Fig 3 When satisfied with shape of dolphin, go over pencil lines with felt-tipped pen. When dry, rub out any unwanted pencil lines. Using pen add dots to make shading on part of the dolphin as indicated.

Colour the dolphins

Let's draw a Grey seal

You will need a soft pencil (2B), paper, eraser and felt-tipped pen.

Fig 1 Draw egg shapes with soft pencil indicating eye, snout, flippers and rock

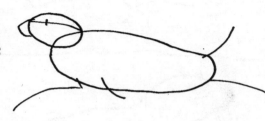

Fig 2 Connect up lines to work up shape of seal

Fig 3 When satisfied with form go over pencil lines with thin marker. When dry rub out unwanted pencil lines. Leave details until last

Colour the Grey Seal

Let's draw a Little Owl

You will need a soft pencil (2B), paper, eraser and felt-tipped pen.

Fig 1 Using a pencil begin by drawing egg shapes. (As shown). Then indicate eyes, bill, legs and wings

Fig 2 Connect up lines adding more detail

Fig 3 When satisfied with own shape go over pencil with felt-tipped pen adding detail as indicated. When dry rub out unwanted pencil lines

Colour the Little Owl

Common in Europe but not found in Ireland. Brought into Britain in the late 19th century. Seen in daylight sitting on poles or walls in open country. Not much bigger than a song-thrush. Brown with bright yellow eyes. Food: earthworms, insects.

NATURE QUIZ

Questions

1. What is a leatherjacket?

2. What is a robber-fly?

3. A fly has four pairs of wings. True or False?

4. Ants, wasps, bees and termites are insects with something in common. What is it?

5. What do bees feed their young on?

6. Caddis-fly, dragonfly, demoiselle, damselfly, mayfly, stonefly, alder-fly have what in common?

7. What is the name given to young dragonflies and mayflies?

8. What is a glow-worm?

Answers on next page

83

Answers

1. The larva of a cranefly (daddy-long-legs).

2. A fly that catches other insects and suck out their juices.

3. False. True flies have only one set of wings.

4. They all live in colonies.

5. On nectar and pollen. (Wasps feed their young on animal food).

6. They all live near or around ponds and streams.

7. Nymphs.

8. A beetle, that can produce a light by using chemicals in its body while flying at night.

Grey Heron

Complete the picture by joining up the dots

MAMMAL QUIZ

These six wild animals can be found in Ireland. Can you name them?

1 Otter

2 RED Squirrell

3 Fox

4 _Stoat_

5 _Badger_

6 _hedgehog_

HOW THE SPIDER CAME INTO THE WORLD

A Greek legend

There was a famous dyer of fabrics called Idmon. He lived at Colophon in Lydia. He had a daughter named Arachne. She was even more famous than her father for she was considered the finest weaver of fabrics and tapestries. Once, while completing one of the most exquisite tapestries she had ever worked on for the temple of Zeus she said proudly,

'Is this not the most beautiful tapestry in the land of Greece? Could any goddess in Mount Olympus make a finer thing than this?'

She showed it to the stars. 'Is this not

perfection itself? I, a mere mortal, have produced something fit for the great god Zeus himself.'

What Arachne didn't know was that Zeus' daughter Athena was sitting on an olive branch, close to her house, in the guise of a little owl.

Athena was furious when she heard the uttering of Arachne.

'How dare she make such a claim, especially in front of me! I who am the patron goddess of female arts and industries!'

That night Arachne went to bed so pleased she had completed this intricate tapestry which would be presented to the temple priests the following day at the ceremony to the god of gods, Zeus. The angry Athena flew into the open window of the workshop, landed on the tapestry and tore it to shreds.

The next morning Arachne awoke to the sound of loud knocking at her bedroom.

'Arachne, Arachne!' her father called as he banged on the door.

Arachne hurried to get dressed, then opened the door.

'Come quick, my child,' said her father. 'A terrible thing has happened.'

She hurried towards the workshop with her father. On opening the door to the workshop she saw the most terrible sight. There on the floor, torn into a thousand pieces, was her beautiful tapestry. She picked up some of the ripped pieces of cloth and wept uncontrollably.

Idmon could not understand how such a terrible thing could happen for the doors to the workshop were locked as it housed such a prized possession.

Arachne ran out of the house shrieking and crying for she could not be consoled or comforted.

Her father hoped after a time her pain would ease. In the meantime he would have to explain what happened to the temple priests.

Arachne had not returned all day, it was getting dark and her father was becoming very anxious. There was a gentle knock at the door. He opened it and there stood an old shepherd.

'I'm sorry to be the bearer of bad tidings but I found your beautiful daughter Arachne dead. I found her hanging from the bough of an olive tree.'

Idmon gave out a loud cry of pain that could even be heard in Mount Olympus. The goddess Athena, hearing the sad cry of Arachne's father, became very remorseful and regretted tearing to pieces the tapestry and causing poor Arachne's death. Athena flew to where Arachne's body swayed in the cold air.

'I will bring you back to life, not as your former self, but as a spider and turn this rope into a web. You will be a creature surpassing all others in the art of weaving and the secret will be passed on to your kind until the end of time.'

And according to legend this is how spiders came into the world.

STRANGE BUT TRUE

* Did you know the scientific name to classify spiders is Arachnida?

* People of old believed that if one was bitten by a tarantula death would follow. So to prevent death you had to listen to music, preferably played by a group of magicians. Not just any music could cure you – it was a certain song or piece of music that worked on an individual, different music for different people depending on their temperament. From a state of fear to sadness, the right music would perk you up, make you dance or sing, then go into a frenzy. Finally you would collapse and when you awoke you would be cured.

* In ancient times some people carried spiders in a bag around their neck to ward off diseases.

* Little Miss Muffet of nursery fame was a real girl. Her father, Dr Thomas Muffet (1533-1604) forced her to eat spiders every day, he believed it was a cure for all ailments.

* Most spiders have eight eyes some only have seven.

FUN TO DO

Recycle that Plastic Bottle

Plastics are made from oil. They are light, tough and resist decay. Here are a few ways to reuse a large plastic bottle.

Design a bird-feeder for your garden or school grounds

Hang it from a tree or large shrub.

Make several holes around the bottle.

Get a stick and push it from one side to the other so that birds can perch.

Fill the bottle with wild-bird food.

Bird Feeder

Make a slug trap

Slugs can be a problem for gardeners so, instead of using harmful slug pellets, cut off the top and bottom of a plastic bottle as shown. Sink your

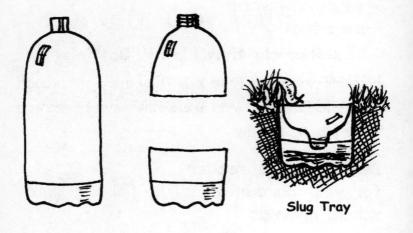

Slug Tray

trap into the soil and fill with beer. Ask an adult for it — this way only slugs are affected.

Grow cress

Cut the base and make a tub to grow your cress.

Grow cress in base of bottle

Growing a plant from seed in a pot

Cut a large section of plastic bottle as shown (make a cloche) and cover the pot with it. This will help protect your plants.

Growing a plant from seed

Grow wildflowers from seeds

Cut a section of the bottle as shown. Fill with potting compost. Sprinkle seeds, cover with compost and lightly water.

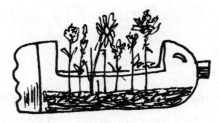

Grow wild flowers from seeds, then plant them outdoors

If you have a lot of plastic contact your local council to find out if they have a recycling scheme for plastic.

Fly Eagle Fly by Don Conroy

Like silence you came
From castle of rocks
Riding the northwind down to the sea
Soaring and gliding on proud stiff wings
Past ancient cliffs
That held your memory, locked in
Her sacred stones

On currents of warm air you sail
Tracing hidden pathways through the sky
Do your wings carry secrets
From mountain to mountain and from
Rivers to the sea?

The earth coloured your body
While the sun burnished your head
Your wild screams tear the silence
As you scan with that fierce stare
Across landscapes that earth bound spirits share

Do not listen to their plea
Or be charmed by their weasal words
They who kill the visions
And dream only empty dreams
They can offer only chains and
Would clip your precious wings
So fly eagle fly
On wings, so free!

EXTINCT

Many birds and mammals have become extinct in Ireland. When an animal becomes extinct it means that the entire population of that animal has died out in a country or throughout the entire world.

The golden eagle became extinct in Ireland in 1912. Great effort has been made by the Irish Raptor Study Group to reintroduce these magnificent birds to their former haunts.

Did you know there are many place-names in Ireland related to the eagle (e.g. Gleneagle in Co. Kerry) or the Irish word for eagle 'iolar' (e.g. Meenanillar in Co. Donegal).

Let's draw a golden eagle

Materials

You will need paper, a HB pencil, a thin felt-tipped marker and an eraser.

Fig 1 let's begin by drawing egg shapes as shown. Indicate where eye, beak and legs should go. Connect head to body and line where tail should be.

Fig 2 add in shapes by joining up lines as shown.

Fig 3 when satisfied with eagle shape, put in some more detail. Go over drawing with thin black marker. When dry rub out unwanted pencil lines.

Fig 4 leave details until last. Put in more feathers and using cross hatching lines go over the body to complete the finished drawing.

BIRDS OF PREY

Birds of prey are birds that prey upon or eat other birds, animals, fish or insects. Therefore birds of prey are carnivores. Birds of prey have powerful talons with sharp claws for grasping their prey, a sharp hooked beak for

tearing at the flesh and large eyes that give excellent vision. Most birds of prey hunt during the day. Birds of prey that hunt during the night are called owls. Birds of prey range in size from tiny falconets (almost as small as sparrows) to the massive vultures, condors and eagles. Kestrels and sparrowhawks are the most common birds of prey in Ireland.

✤ What did the lion say when he saw the two hunters on bicycles? Meals on wheels.

✤ One man said to another: ' I've lost my dog.'
Second man: 'Put an ad in the newspapers.'
First man: 'Don't be crazy, dogs can't read.'

✤ A man bought a parrot at an auction and said to the auctioneer: 'Are you sure this parrot can talk? I've bid a great deal of money.'
Auctioneer: 'Of course he can. Who do you think was bidding against you.'

✤ Woman: 'Do you sell cat's meat?'
Butcher: 'Only if you can pay for it.'

✤ A man was going to buy a guard-dog when he noticed the dog had no teeth.
'What's the point of a guard-dog with no teeth?' he complained to the owner.
The owner replied: 'It may have no teeth but it can give a terrible suck.'

FOSSILS
SECRETS OF THE PAST

FOSSILS ARE AMAZING! FOSSIL MEANS THE TRACES OF ANY PAST LIFE PRESERVED IN THE ROCKS. SO A FOSSIL RECORD AS SEEN BELOW IS THE PHYSICAL PROOF OF THE EXISTENCE OF DINOSAURS LEFT BEHIND IN ROCKS.

How are fossils made?
* WHEN AN ANIMAL DIES, THE FLESH ROTS AWAY LEAVING ONLY BONES.
* BONES GET BURIED UNDER MUD, SAND OR ROTTING VEGETATION.
* OVER MILLIONS OF YEARS THESE BONES SOAK UP MINERALS FROM THE ROCKS AROUND THEM.
* THE BONES EVENTUALLY BECOME ROCK. THEY ARE FOSSILISED!

Fossil of an Allosaurus skull

ALLOSAURUS
(MEANS 'OTHER REPTILE'
* A MEAT-EATER.
* LIVED 156-130 MILLION YEARS AGO IN COLORADO, NEW MEXICO, TANZANIA AND AUSTRALIA.
* LENGTH: 11M (36FT)
* WEIGHT: 2 TONNES

Palaeontology is the study of fossils. Fossils include dinosaurs and ammonites. Some fossils are so tiny they can only be seen through a microscope or magnifying glass. People who study these fossils are called micro-palaeontologists.

Some of these fossils are called foraminifera. They are found on rocky shores or out on the sea-bed. Some date back 560 million years.

STRANGE BUT TRUE

One of the world's rarest dinosaur finds was discovered after spending decades as a paperweight on a university professor's desk. The piece of skin was embedded in a lump of rock. It was identified after the professor died. Only four other samples were found world-wide.

How to draw hands

Here are a few guidelines on how to draw hands.
Follow these easy steps to draw open and closed hands

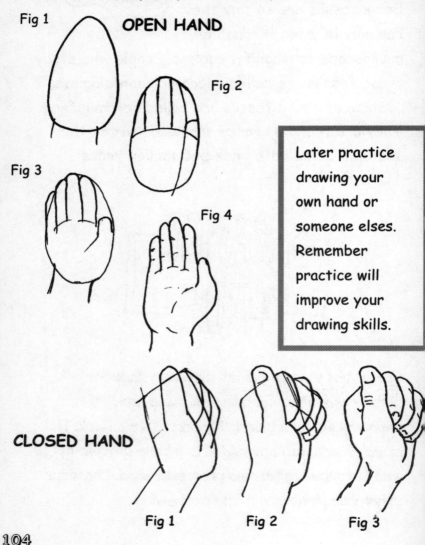

OPEN HAND

Fig 1

Fig 2

Fig 3

Fig 4

Later practice drawing your own hand or someone elses. Remember practice will improve your drawing skills.

CLOSED HAND

Fig 1   Fig 2   Fig 3

How to draw a kitten

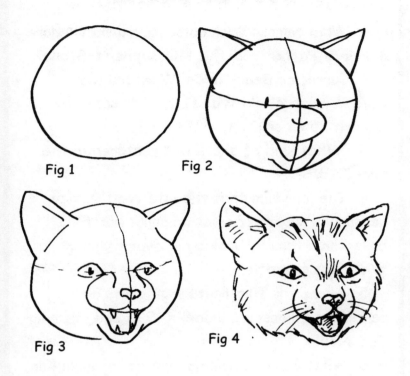

Fig 1

Fig 2

Fig 3

Fig 4

Fig 1 Draw a circle using a soft pencil (HB or 2B)

Fig 2 Add in ears, eyes, and mouth as shown.

Fig 3 Add in more detail

Fig 4 Go over pencil drawing with a felt-tipped marker. When dry rub out any unwanted pencil lines. Put in finish details.

MOVIE QUIZ

1 What famous Irish actor played Dumbledore in **Harry Potter and the Philosopher's Stone**?

2 Curracloe Beach in Co. Wexford was used in what World War II film directed by Steven Spielberg?

3 What kind of shark was featured in the film JAWS?

4 The last film that the late Walt Disney personally supervised was an animation film based on a famous book by Rudyard Kipling. What was the title?

5 Name the film featuring genetically re-created dinosaurs made in 1993 and starring Sam Neill.

6 What was the name of the young male lion in the animated film **The Lion King** (1994)?

7 Name the film about an otter based on a book by Henry Williamson.

8 Edgar Rice Burroughs wrote several books about this lord of the jungle and there have been many films featuring him. Who is he?

ANSWERS ON NEXT PAGE

Answers

1. Richard Harris
2. Saving Private Ryan
3. A great white shark
4. The Jungle Book
5. Jurassic Park
6. Simba
7. Tarka the Otter
8. Tarzan

Barn Owl
Ghost of the Night

As twilight falls upon the ruin
A blackbird scolds departing light
While woodcock roding at the moon
And bats take flight
Those messengers of night.

A meditative silence around me crept
A silence so intense -
Had the world stopped to rest?

Alone I waited
With excitement and care.
For beware the castle lore
Of the demons and the ghosts
That stalk the night once more.

From out of dwellings dark
Came a hissing and a snoring
Then a shriek! My heart did leap.
No ghost or shade I saw
On silent winged flight
But a beautiful white bird of night
Who made his home
Where king or squire once did rest.